The Public Record Office
SOUVENIR
GUIDE

PRO PUBLICATIONS

Introduction

PASSENGERS IN THE trains that pass over Kew Bridge towards Richmond may look to their left and wonder what the complex of large buildings set in a landscape of ponds and gardens might be. Few people will connect it with the sign at Kew Gardens, the next station: 'Alight here for the Public Record Office.' Yet in this quiet suburban setting lies that most secret of gardens, the treasure house of the nation's memory – the National Archives.

Its records span a thousand years of recorded history, and in 1998 filled 167 kilometres of shelving: literally millions of papers, parchments, maps, plans and photographs – even objects as varied as medieval coin dies and samples of nineteenth-century buttons. The documents illustrated in this *Souvenir Guide* can provide no more than a taste of that wealth of material, a few nuggets culled from one of the world's richest seams of history in the raw. Anyone who comes to search the records will testify that mining those seams can be hard labour, and even dirty work if it involves touching something that might not have been looked at for centuries; but making new discoveries can be deeply rewarding, whether it be about kings and queens, statesmen and generals, or the seaman or soldier who may be your ancestor.

The buildings at Kew have only been open to the public since 1977, and in 1995 the site was significantly extended when the concrete brutalism of the earlier offices was linked to the airy spaciousness of the later ones by a lofty atrium that forms

Opposite: The Court of King Louis XI of France, 1476. From a copy of the statutes which established the Order of St Michael. E 36/276

The Public Record Office at Kew.
© Hugh Alexander 1998

Below: Detail from Nelson's funeral procession, 8 January 1806. LC 2/40

the main entrance. Before its move to Kew the Public Record Office had a number of sites, the most important of which, in Chancery Lane in central London, closed in 1997. It had stored records of government since the fourteenth century, and Samuel Pepys in his diary notes a visit there in 1669: 'I hired a clerk there to read to me about twelve or more rolls which I did call for; and it was great pleasure to me to see the method wherein their Rolles are kept.' When the Chancery Lane site finally closed, a new office in central London, the Family Records Centre in Islington, was opened. There you may see copies on microfilm of many of the most popular records consulted by genealogists – notably the nineteenth-century population census returns – as well as indexes to the post-1837 civil registers of births, marriages and deaths held by the Office for National Statistics.

Above: The Public Record Office in Chancery Lane during the Blitz. View from Fleet Street, 30 December 1940. PRO 50/59

Left: Preserving the documents. This Exchequer enrolment contains numerous sheets of parchment (sheepskin) sewn head to tail.

Left: Medieval tally sticks. E 402/347

Below: Tally stick design for the gates at the Ruskin Avenue entrance to the Public Record Office.

Links with the medieval past of the Public Record Office and with its Chancery Lane site are preserved at Kew. The ironwork at the main entrance and on the bridge over the twin ponds – these act as balancing reservoirs as well as being home to the Office's own flock of swans – carry a design of medieval tally sticks, which were used by officials to record accounts. The slates in the paving and garden wall were formerly fireproof shelves that were installed in the nineteenth-century Chancery Lane repository; the slate itself comes from Valencia island off the coast of Ireland, which also provided slates for the roof of the Houses of Parliament. The early eighteenth-century lead cisterns on either side of the

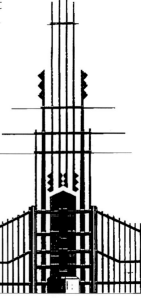

revolving doors into the building are from houses that once fronted Chancery Lane.

The Public Record Office, founded in 1838, responsible to the Lord Chancellor and now an executive agency of government, has four main roles:

■ supervising the selection, safekeeping and transfer of public records created by government departments and courts;
■ keeping records selected for preservation in carefully controlled environmental conditions in perpetuity;
■ providing public access to the records and promoting their use;
■ advising government and other bodies, international and local, on records issues.

Some records, such as the censuses, may be closed for up to one hundred years to protect the privacy of the individuals named in them, but most may be read by the public once they are thirty years old. Through its Archives Direct 2001 Programme, the Office will put key catalogues on its web site, along with a virtual museum of its treasures. The web site address is: **http://www.pro.gov.uk/**

Bringing the archives to life – the Education Service at work.
© Hugh Alexander 1997

FURTHER READING

Amanda Bevan (ed), *Tracing Your Ancestors in the Public Record Office*, PRO Publications, January 1999. The fifth edition of this guide has been revised and updated to include new accessions, clearer descriptions of the records and illustrations.

John D Cantwell, *The Public Record Office 1838–1958*, HMSO, 1991. The authoritative history of the Office from its foundation to 1958, this covers in particular the vital part played by successive deputy keepers and masters of the rolls.

Jane Cox, *Never Been Here Before?*, PRO Publications, 1997. A new guide to the Family Records Centre in London.

Jane Cox, *New to Kew?*, PRO Publications, 1997. The essential first-time guide for anyone wishing to research their own family history at the Public Record Office at Kew.

Aidan Lawes, *Chancery Lane 1377–1977*, PRO Publications, 1996. An illustrated history of the site associated with public records for over 600 years, this popular history examines through documents, anecdotes and oral history how and why the national archives developed.

Domesday Book and Magna Carta

MEDIEVAL MONARCHS PRIZED their most important documents as highly as their gold and jewels and cared for them in the same way. They were kept in royal treasuries such as the one at Winchester, or accompanied the king when he travelled his realm. Domesday Book, a detailed survey of England made twenty years after the Norman Conquest, is Britain's oldest public record and the greatest treasure of the Public Record Office. For centuries, it was used as legal proof of title to land and, above all, of the rights of the king. In contrast, Magna Carta, that other key icon of medieval history, defined certain rights of the subject against the king. The re-issue of 1225, ten years after King John gave way to his baronial opponents at Runnymede, is regularly carried in procession at the Magna Carta celebrations. These are held every three years in rotation at the sites associated with the original 1215 charter – of which only four sealed copies now survive, two at the British Library, one in Lincoln Cathedral and one in Salisbury Cathedral.

Domesday Book, 1086

County by county, manor by manor, and landowner by landowner, Domesday Book lists how much land there was, the number of ploughs, mills, fisheries, vineyards, even animals, and the taxable value of the land before and after the Conquest. William the Conqueror commissioned the survey in October 1085, and it was substantially completed in 1086. Originally known as the book of Winchester after its place of safekeeping, it is really two volumes: Great Domesday and Little Domesday. E 31/2

Domesday Chest, c.15th century

Traditionally stored in this locked chest (which even has its own reference number) from the 17th century, Domesday Book is still kept under lock and key at the Public Record Office. An exact copy is on display in the entrance to the building.
E 31/4

Magna Carta

Magna Carta was issued by John in 1215 and re-issued a year later on his death in the name of his son, Henry III, but with significant omissions relevant to national liberties and taxation. It was re-issued twice more – in 1217, again with some changes, and in 1225 (left). This is one of three surviving examples, and is the final, definitive form of the charter of liberties, which entered the statute books as the first and most fundamental statement of English rights, granted under the seal of King Henry III.
DL 10/71

This extract (left) from the Great Domesday volume shows a typical entry – that for Norton, within the Hundred of Hodnet, in the county of Shropshire. It was held by Helgot, or Helgo, a prominent Norman follower of Earl Roger, King William's cousin. The entry reads:

In HODNET Hundred Helgot holds NORTON (in Hales) from Earl Roger. Azor held it; he was a free man. 3 hides which pay tax. Land for 6 ploughs.
1 rider with 1 plough;
4 villagers with 2 ploughs. Woodland for fattening 200 pigs. Value in the time of King Edward [the Confessor], 30 shillings; now 20 shillings. E 31/2/2

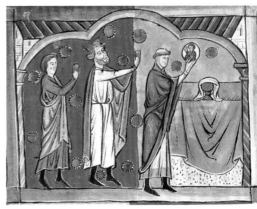

Edward the Confessor

When Edward died on 5 January 1066 there were three claimants to the throne of England: Harold Godwinson, the most powerful English earl; Harald Hardrada, king of Norway; and William, duke of Normandy. Harold fought off Hardrada at the battle of Stamford Bridge in the north of England, but was defeated by William, and killed, at the battle of Hastings in October that year – almost twenty years before the Conqueror ordered the survey that was to become Domesday Book. This illumination – depicting Edward and Earl Leofric at mass seeing a vision of Christ in the Eucharist – is from a 13th-century abbreviated version of Domesday Book, known as the *Abbreviatio*.
E 36/284

The Middle Ages

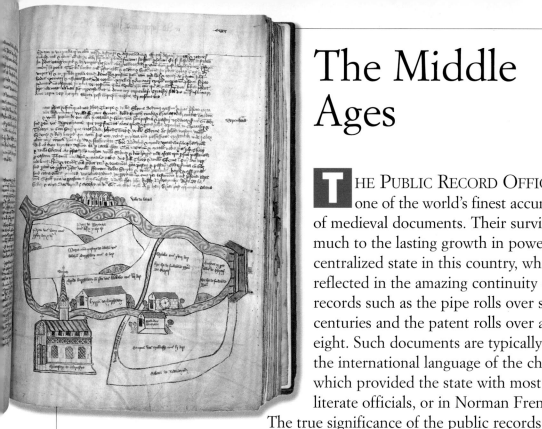

THE PUBLIC RECORD OFFICE has one of the world's finest accumulations of medieval documents. Their survival owes much to the lasting growth in power of the centralized state in this country, which is reflected in the amazing continuity of serial records such as the pipe rolls over seven centuries and the patent rolls over almost eight. Such documents are typically in Latin, the international language of the church, which provided the state with most of its literate officials, or in Norman French.

The true significance of the public records lies in these long unbroken series. Often interrelated, they provide historians with a richness and depth that can be lacking in artificial collections of isolated examples of individual 'famous' documents.

Chertsey Abbey
Map, 15th century. Chertsey in Surrey was one of many Benedictine abbeys in England. Medieval picture maps like this are rare – this one was drawn to settle a dispute over pasture rights. E 164/25

Coins
Coin die from the York ecclesiastical mint, c. 1377. This 14th-century die was sent to the royal Treasury when it became worn through use and had to be replaced. Blank discs of metal were placed between two dies, each bearing an impression of one side of the coin, which were struck with a hammer. E 29/1/43

Medieval Jews
Anti-Semitic cartoon on a Jewish receipt roll, 13th century. The only significant religious and racial minority in England, Jews were protected by King John and his successors who saw them as a source of wealth and taxed them heavily. But in 1290 Edward I withdrew that protection and they were expelled from England. E 401/1565

France and England
Ratification of treaty with Francis I of France concerning ecclesiastical affairs, 1527. This detail depicts a meeting of cardinals and other churchmen. The treaty was signed by Cardinal Wolsey, Henry VIII's Lord Chancellor and the last of the great line of medieval churchmen who administered both church and state.
E 30/1114

Pipe roll
The pipe rolls, in which sheriffs – the king's key officials in the counties – accounted for revenue due to the Crown at annual audits, run in an unbroken series for almost seven centuries, from 1156 until 1833.
E 372/445

Henry II
Charter of Henry II, c. 1155–60. This confirms an earlier grant to Holy Trinity priory, London, for £25 to be paid annually out of the rents of the city of Exeter. The seal has been used as the basis for the Public Record Office's logo. E 42/527

Kings and Queens

MOST DEPICTIONS OF royalty in the public records are icons of power – the great seals of state or illuminated portraits on certain plea rolls – and more informal portraiture had to await the age of the camera. Many thousands of warrants bear hastily scribbled royal signatures, but some kings, such as Henry VII, laboriously examined and initialled detailed accounts of royal revenues. Few official documents, however, reveal the true character of the man or woman behind the image. Even letters like the one written by Elizabeth I as a schoolgirl held up a formal mask to the world. Kings or queens who displayed traits that were too human might lay themselves open to caricature and ridicule. Those who overstepped the conventional role of what was expected of the monarch might face in one century, execution; in another, the requirement to abdicate.

Seal of Elizabeth I
The second great seal of Elizabeth I, 1586–1603. The inscription reads: *Elizabetha dei gracia Anglie Francie et Hibernie Regina Fidei Defensor* ('Elizabeth, by grace of God, Queen of England, France and Ireland, Defender of the Faith'). The seal matrix was engraved by the famous miniaturist Nicholas Hilliard.
SC 13/N3

The young Elizabeth
Letter to Catherine Parr, 1547. The only one of Henry VIII's wives to survive him, Catherine Parr had secretly married the ambitious Thomas Seymour, Lord Seymour of Sudeley. The future queen, then 14 years old, wrote this letter after Catherine sent her away from the Seymour household lest malicious rumours start to circulate about Elizabeth's relationship with her stepmother's new husband. SP 10/2

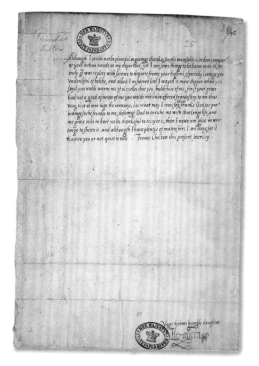

Edward VIII
Edward VIII's letter of abdication, 1936. The king's renunciation of the throne was precipitated by the divorce of Wallis Simpson from her second husband. Edward refused to bow to pressure from the establishment to abandon their marriage plans, and became the only British monarch to abdicate. PC 11/1

Henry VIII

Valor Ecclesiasticus, 1535. This survey and valuation of all ecclesiastical benefices in England and Wales was carried out as part of Henry VIII's effective 'nationalization' of the Church of England: the first of more than 800 monasteries were suppressed in 1536. This image shows the king at the height of his powers. E 344/22

George V

An informal photograph, 1903. The face of the future George V, then the Prince of Wales, is illuminated by a match as he lights a cigarette.
Photographer: Robert Johnson.
COPY 1/466

Mary Queen of Scots

Allegorical sketch, c. June 1567. Mary is depicted as a mermaid, a symbol of prostitution. She had lost popular support when she married James, earl of Bothwell, who was widely believed to have killed her first husband, Lord Darnley. She was executed on 8 February 1587. SP 52/13

Famous Names

FAMOUS PEOPLE APPEAR in the public records for much the same reasons as less well-known ones. Some are there because they worked for the government, often in unexpected capacities: Geoffrey Chaucer, Daniel Defoe, Robert Burns and William Wordsworth were all – surprisingly – tax or customs collectors. Others, even if they did not work for the state, are almost certainly recorded as taxpayers, alive or dead. Legal records and wills can be a rich source of information about figures like William Shakespeare, John Milton and William Morris.

Elton John
Entry in change of name deed register, 6 January 1972. Reginald Kenneth Dwight became the better-known singer and musician Elton (Hercules) John when he renounced, relinquished and abandoned the use of his former name.
J 18/458

William Shakespeare
Detail from the playwright's will, 25 March 1616 (far right). This signature and two others are believed to be the only surviving examples of Shakespeare's handwriting. The bulk of his property was left to his daughter, Susanna Hall; he bequeathed his wife, Anne Hathaway, his second-best bed. The sketch (right) is of a portrait, said to be contemporary, endorsed (in Italian) 'Shakespeare. Playwright, Englishman. London 21st July 1604', and brought back to Venice by the then Venetian ambassador Nicolo Molin in 1606.

The sketch itself dates from the 19th century and was made by an editor who had been employed by the Public Record Office to make copies of state papers in Venice.
PROB 1/4; PRO 30/25/205

Lord Nelson

Depiction of Nelson's funeral procession, 8 January 1806. Nelson's coffin was brought back to England after the battle of Trafalgar and carried from Greenwich to Whitehall Stairs 'in one of the greatest Aquatic Processions that ever was beheld on the River Thames'. His death on 21 October 1805 is recorded in the log of HMS *Victory* (left) alongside the names of members of his crew who also died in the battle.

LC 2/40; ADM 52/3711

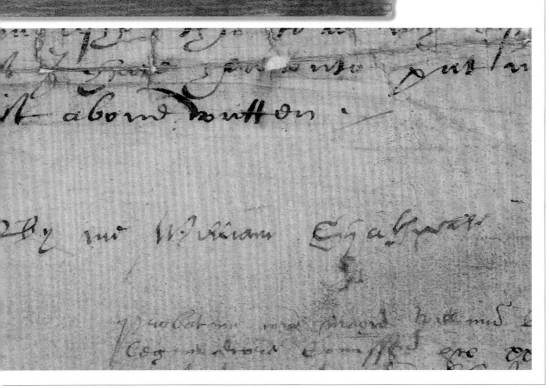

Ramsay MacDonald and Charles Chaplin

Chequers, 1931. Ramsay MacDonald (right), the first Labour prime minister, strolls through the grounds of his official country residence with Charlie Chaplin, showing there is nothing new in the mixing of senior politicians with stars from the silver screen.

PRO 30/69/1666

The Individual and the State

TAXES, LIKE DEATH, affect rich and poor alike. Detailed lists of taxpayers from the Middle Ages to the late seventeenth century survive, but may provide little more than names and an indication of relative wealth and status. Evidence given in legal disputes can provide rich insights into the life of ordinary people. The nineteenth-century population census returns are the most comprehensive records. They were meant to include the entire population – not even Queen Victoria was exempt – although, then as now, there were some who escaped the net. They are the most heavily used records in the Office, so much so that they would long ago have crumbled into dust had they not been microfilmed.

Family historians who study records such as these account for over half the users of the Public Record Office.

Royalty
Census return, 1851. Victoria was simply entered as 'Queen' under the heading Rank, Profession or Occupation. Since 1801 all national censuses have been carried out every ten years with the exception of 1941. The information is confidential and the records are closed to the public for one hundred years. HO 107/1478

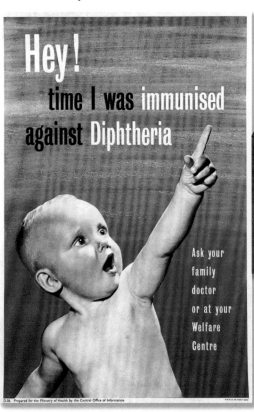

Children
Central Office of Information poster, 1957. In 1948 the state assumed new responsibility for the health care of all its citizens in setting up the Welfare State. This poster urges the benefits of immunizing babies against diphtheria. The campaigns have been so successful that the disease is now rare in the United Kingdom.
INF 13/292/28

Merchant seamen
'CR 10' cards from the Register of Seamen, 1918–21. These are from a central register that recorded all seamen on merchant ships, and form a special index

Women

Recruitment poster, Ministry of Information, 1939–45. Women were called upon to work in factories as a patriotic act when men left their jobs to serve king and country in the armed forces.
INF 13/126/6

Taxes

Hearth tax return, 1666. The Great Fire of London started in the bakery of Thomas Farrinor, here recorded (right-hand page, 9th entry) as having five hearths and one oven, in Pudding Lane in September 1666. It lasted for five days and virtually destroyed the city.
E 179/252/32

WOMEN OF BRITAIN
COME INTO THE FACTORIE
SK AT ANY EMPLOYMENT EXCHANGE FOR ADVICE AND FULL DET

made by a 1918 Order under the Defence of the Realm Act. Unlike most cards from other indexes they include photographs, and probably recorded the issuing of identity certificates. They are being microfilmed into the record class BT 364.

Warfare

THE VIOLENCE OF war has been described as the midwife of history. Records give graphic testimony of its fundamental effects on our ancestors – and show how it speeded up the rate of technological advance in the quest for ever more deadly weapons. English, Welsh, Irish and Scots helped to form one of the world's most professional fighting forces, on land and sea, and from the late eighteenth century the service records of some army and navy pensioners even included descriptions of what they looked like. Recently released army service records from the First World War are among the most popular documents in the Office.

Agincourt
Indenture of Robert de Radclyf of Osbalderston, 23 April 1415. In it, Robert agreed that he and two archers would serve Henry V on the expedition to France that culminated in the battle of Agincourt. Their daily wages would be one shilling for himself and sixpence for his men; the king would receive a fixed share of any profits they made from booty or ransoms. E 101/69/6

Cape soldier
Soldier of the Cape of Good Hope Regiment, 1808. The British Army was supplemented by many colonial regiments in the 18th and 19th centuries. A Mounted Rifle Corps was also raised from the Cape.
CO 48/3

The Red Baron
Combat report, 21 April 1918. Captain A R Brown of 209 Squadron of the Royal Air Force claimed to have shot down the red Fokker triplane of Manfred von Richthofen. The notorious 'Red Baron' had been responsible for over eighty 'kills' of Allied aircraft and men.
AIR 1/1228/204/5/2634/2095

Air raid
Photograph, 25 April 1945. Two RAF Lancaster bombers take part in a raid on coastal batteries on Wangerooge island off north-west Germany. It was one of the last sorties of World War II: Germany surrendered less than two weeks later, on 7 May.
AIR 14/3647

Battleship

Ministry of Information poster, 1939–45. It shows the bow and forward guns of a George V Class Royal Navy battleship. Battleships provided the heavy firepower in World War II's most famous battles. The role of the *Duke of York* in the sinking of the *Scharnhorst* on 26 December 1943 is an example. Battleships have been superseded by aircraft-carriers.

INF 3/1651

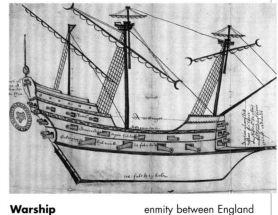

Warship

Depiction of Spanish frigate, 16th–17th century. In 1588 the enmity between England and Spain culminated in the attempted conquest of England by the Spanish Armada. The fleet of 130 ships and 30,000 men was defeated by a combination of English tactics and bad weather. SP 9/205

The Sudan

Heroes of the siege of Khartoum, 1885. Major-General Charles Gordon (centre) withstood Muslim forces led by the Mahdi for ten months. He was killed when they stormed his garrison two days before troops led by Lord Kitchener raised the siege.

Artist: C Fesch. COPY 1/72

Welsh archer

Marginal drawing from a catalogue of records, 13th century. The pictogram of a Welsh archer shows at a glance that the text concerned Wales. A copy of the image was made on the lid of the coffer holding the documents to help identify the contents quickly. E 36/274

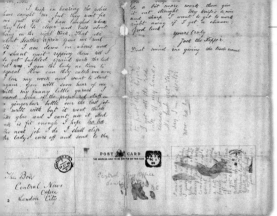

Crime and Punishment

THE PUBLIC RECORD OFFICE has rich holdings of legal records, from those of the local Assize courts, which dealt with capital felonies like murder, burglary, rape and arson, to those of the powerful central courts at Westminster. Many offences were punishable by hanging – a penalty extended in the 'enlightened' eighteenth century to stealing fruit from trees. Transporting criminals to America and later to Australia was common from the seventeenth to the mid-nineteenth centuries, often as an alternative to hanging. The Office also holds the records of many famous treason trials, including those of Sir Thomas More, Anne Boleyn and Guy Fawkes, all of whom were executed. Some mysteries on the files – the Whitechapel murders of 1888 are an example – remain unsolved to this day.

'Jack the Ripper'
Letter and postcard to news agency, September–October 1888. 'Jack the Ripper' murdered six prostitutes in London's East End between August and November 1888. The original correspondence was sent on to Scotland Yard. When the Metropolitan Police published these facsimiles there was a flood of post from hoaxers claiming to be the notorious serial killer. MEPO 3/142

Robin Hood
Account for the wages of the porters of the King's Chamber, November 1324. One of the porters is a certain 'Robyn Hod', who was at this point retired because he could no longer work. His 'golden handshake' amounted to twenty days' wages. Some have argued that this was the 'real' Robin Hood. E 101/380/4

Pentonville prison
Treadmill, 1895. Arrows – symbolizing government property – can be seen on the prisoners' uniforms. First devised in 1818, treadmills were used to discipline convicts or as part of hard labour.
Photographer: William Grove.
COPY 1/420

PLAN AND SECTIONS OF THE GALLOWS

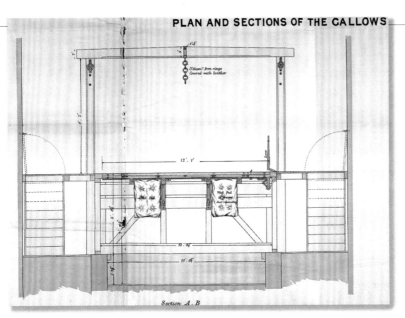

Section A. B

Gallows

Plan of the gallows at Newgate gaol, c. 1880. The last woman to have been hanged was Ruth Ellis on 13 July 1955 at Holloway prison; the last men were John Walby and Peter Allen, at Strangeways gaol, Manchester, on 13 August 1964. Capital punishment for murder was finally abolished in Britain in 1969.
HO 144/18/46327

Guy Fawkes

Signatures, 1605. Guy (Guido) Fawkes signed two confessions. It is believed that the lower example was signed after torture. He was hanged, drawn and quartered for his part in the Gunpowder Plot to blow up the Houses of Parliament. SP 14/216

Oscar Wilde

The marquess of Queensberry's visiting card, 18 February 1895. The marquess left this at the Albemarle Club near Piccadilly. The (misspelt) message reads 'For Oscar Wilde posing Somdomite' and provoked Wilde into initiating the libel proceedings that brought about his downfall. CRIM 1/41/6

Child convict

Photograph taken at Oxford Castle magistrates court, 1870. Julia Ann Crumpling, aged 7, was sentenced to seven days' hard labour for stealing a perambulator.
PCOM 2/352

Politics and Protest

'Black Friday'
Daily Mirror photograph, 1910. The suffragette Ada Wright collapsed in front of the Houses of Parliament on 18 November 1910, when more than 300 members of the Women's Social and Political Union tried to gain entry to the House of Commons.
Photographer: Victor Consolé.
COPY 1/551

THE ORIGINS OF the 'mother of Parliaments' in the thirteenth century, its development and its relationship with the Crown are comprehensively documented in the Public Record Office's holdings. In particular, the Parliament rolls are the nearest thing we have to Hansard for the Middle Ages; although the content changes, the series runs from 1327 to the present day. This continuity is reflected in the series of election writs that survive from 1275. Until the mid-nineteenth century, only a minority of the population was entitled to elect Members of Parliament and women were excluded from voting until 1918. In their campaign for the vote, suffragettes resorted to demonstrations, propaganda, hunger strikes and even violence. Violent direct action was the traditional means of political protest for the disenfranchised and records of its suppression are in state papers, Home Office files and police records.

Parliament
Election writs, 1275 (above) and 1979 (right). Edward I summoned the lords of the realm to the first Parliament in 1275; 700 years later, calling an election is the prerogative of the government of the day. The 1979 writ is for Margaret Thatcher's Finchley constituency in the election that brought her to power as prime minister.
C 219/1/1; C 219/353

Received the within Writ on the *Ninth* day of *April* 1979

En Bennett
Acting Returning Officer

I hereby certify that the Member elected for the *Barnet, Finchley* Constituency in pursuance of the within written Writ is *Margaret Hilda Thatcher* of *19, Flood Street* in the County of *London S.W.3.*

En Bennett
Acting Returning Officer

E N BENNETT

RECEIVED IN CROWN OFFICE
-4 MAY 1979
A.M. 3.15 p.m.
IN CHANCERY

Poor Law
Poster, c. 1837 (right). In 1834 the Poor Law Amendment Act sought to reduce the cost of social welfare to the public purse by forcing the poor into residential workhouses. This poster shows the strength of popular feeling against an Act that provoked widespread rioting.
HO 44/27

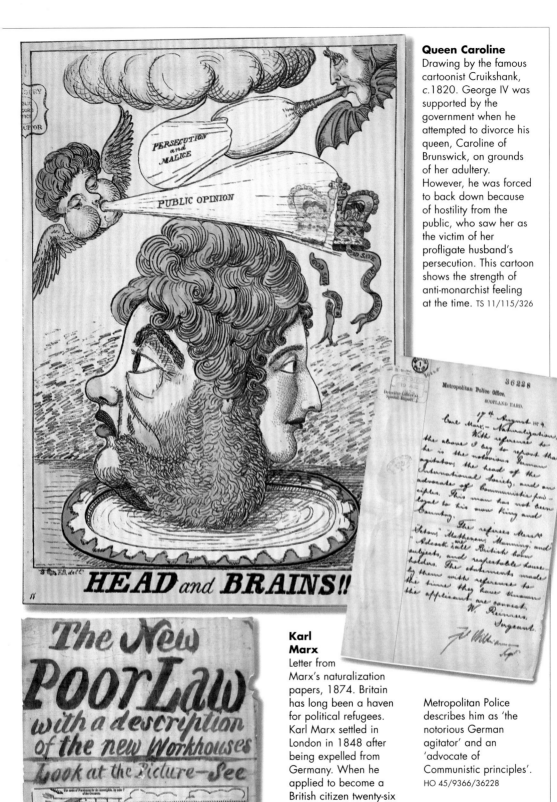

HEAD and BRAINS!!

Queen Caroline

Drawing by the famous cartoonist Cruikshank, c.1820. George IV was supported by the government when he attempted to divorce his queen, Caroline of Brunswick, on grounds of her adultery. However, he was forced to back down because of hostility from the public, who saw her as the victim of her profligate husband's persecution. This cartoon shows the strength of anti-monarchist feeling at the time. TS 11/115/326

Karl Marx

Letter from Marx's naturalization papers, 1874. Britain has long been a haven for political refugees. Karl Marx settled in London in 1848 after being expelled from Germany. When he applied to become a British citizen twenty-six years later his application was refused. Here a sergeant in the Metropolitan Police describes him as 'the notorious German agitator' and an 'advocate of Communistic principles'. HO 45/9366/36228

Architecture, Invention and Design

Computer
Colossus, 1943. Early computers were developed to help crack German signals intelligence during World War II. This prototype, known as Colossus, was used at Bletchley Park, Buckinghamshire.
FO 850/234

PATENT, DESIGN AND trademark registers attest to the extraordinary range of inventiveness and design skills of the British, as much yesterday as today. From the late sixteenth century inventors could protect their right to exploit their inventions commercially by applying for letters patent which gave them a monopoly on the design or specification for a fixed period. From the 1730s, specifications – plans and drawings – were also enrolled for legal protection. The Public Record Office holds such patents up to 1853. Manufactured goods like metalwork, pottery and fabric were not fully protected until 1839, when copies of such designs could be deposited with the registrar of designs; these records, up to 1910, are now in the Office. There are also innumerable architectural plans and drawings for buildings, from humble village schools to royal palaces, that the state commissioned or subsidized.

Paper cut-outs
Victorian fashion, 1885. The clothes are designed to be cut out and fixed to figures, with tabs.
Artist: A Baker. COPY 1/67

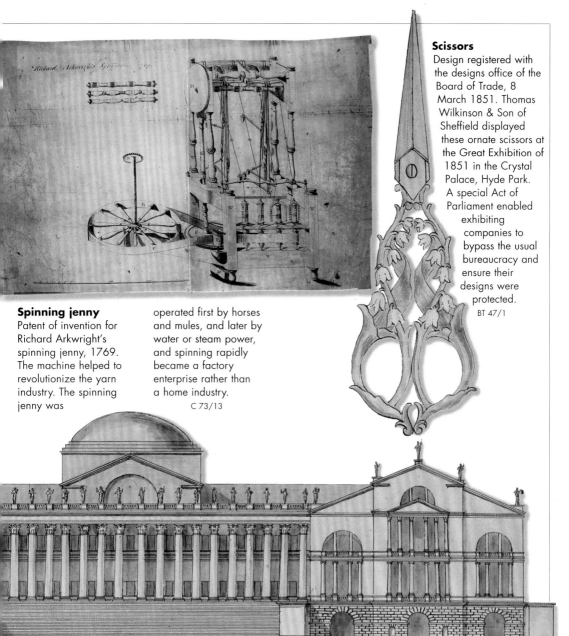

Scissors

Design registered with the designs office of the Board of Trade, 8 March 1851. Thomas Wilkinson & Son of Sheffield displayed these ornate scissors at the Great Exhibition of 1851 in the Crystal Palace, Hyde Park. A special Act of Parliament enabled exhibiting companies to bypass the usual bureaucracy and ensure their designs were protected.
BT 47/1

Spinning jenny

Patent of invention for Richard Arkwright's spinning jenny, 1769. The machine helped to revolutionize the yarn industry. The spinning jenny was operated first by horses and mules, and later by water or steam power, and spinning rapidly became a factory enterprise rather than a home industry.
C 73/13

Architecture

Elevation for the Houses of Parliament, 1739. Lord Burlington, a patron of literature and the arts, who was responsible for the building of Chiswick House in London in 1730–6, entered this design in a competition for a new Houses of Parliament. It was never built. WORK 29/3358

Wallpaper

Wallpaper pattern, 23 December 1839. Registered by William Evans of Shoreditch, London, this was among the first designs to receive legal protection.
BT 42/14

King's messenger
King's Remembrancer account, 1360. Messengers kept the monarch in touch with his officials and diplomatic representatives. This graffito appears in a list of envoys' expenses.
E 101/309/11

Transport

CHANGING MODES OF transport, from the horses used by medieval kings on royal progress to the evolving design of ships built for the Royal Navy, are fully and often graphically reflected in the public records. Railway companies are recorded here because of their nationalization earlier this century. Posters and designs are also useful sources of information. Inquiries into disasters like the sinking of the *Titanic* are a reminder that technological progress has never been infallible.

The *Titanic*
One of the last telegrams sent from the SS *Titanic*, 14–15 April 1912. Jack Phillips (right), the wireless operator, went down with the ship after sending this message which was picked up by the Russian steamer SS *Birma*. MT 9/920C; COPY 1/566

The Russian East Asiatic S.S. Co.   Radio-Telegram.

S.S. "Birma".

| No. words. | Origin. Station. | Time handed in. | Via. | Remarks. |

6307   S.

to   Titanic   about
1-40 a.m.

C/O   SOS SOS CQD CQD = MGY

We are sinking fast passengers being put into boats

MGY

Trains
Idealized London railway station as realized by the Ministry of Information, 1939–45. The first

Airship

Royal Navy airship HMA No 6, 1915. Vickers acquired the rights for the design of the airship, here undergoing trials at Barrow, from a German company. Early in World War I Britain and Germany both used airships for maritime reconnaissance.

AIR 1/728/176/3/38

Dock

Floating dock, 1899. Made from steel pontoons, a floating dock sinks below the level of the ship that is being repaired when the pontoons are filled with water and rises, lifting the ship with it, when they are emptied. Here a Royal Navy ship tows a floating dock off Bermuda. ADM 195/5

Motor show

Poster for Automobile Club Show, Richmond, 1899. Motor cars were a relatively new form of transport; the Act that required a man carrying a red flag to walk in front of a self-propelled vehicle had been repealed only three years before this exhibition was held.

COPY 1/149

passenger steam-locomotive railway, from Stockton to Darlington, opened in 1837; a hundred years later train travel was so much a part of life that it featured in 'The British Scene' series of paintings.

Artist: Grace Golden.

INF 3/1740

Britain and North America

IN 1584 SIR WALTER RALEIGH was first granted letters patent to discover and colonize 'remote and barbarous landes' in the name of Elizabeth I, and in 1585 colonizers settled on Roanoke Island, in what is now North Carolina. This colony failed. The first permanent British settlement, founded in 1607, was Jamestown; named after the reigning king, James I, it was in the state of Virginia, named after his predecessor, Elizabeth I, the Virgin Queen. The Public Record Office is particularly rich in records relating to early colonial America and there is ample evidence of how close the two countries have remained – so close that twentieth-century scholars may study United States foreign policy through British assessments.

Jamestown
List of burgesses elected to the first assembly at 'James city', 30 July 1619. Jamestown was founded by the Virginia Company of London, which had been granted a charter to establish colonies in America. CO 1/1

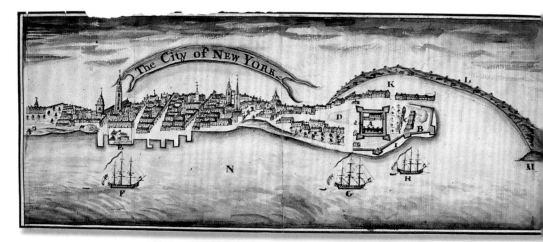

New York
Map of New York and Fort St George, 1 November 1765. The city was at that time governed by Britain, and Royal Navy ships are shown in the harbour.
Artist: W Cockburn. MPI 68

Yalta conference
Churchill, Roosevelt and Stalin at the Yalta conference, February 1945. The meeting was crucial in shaping post-war Europe, and saw the Soviet Union agreeing to enter the war against Japan and to join the United Nations. INF 14/447

Pocahontas

One of the first maps of Virginia, 1608. Pocahontas (top right), a native North American princess, is said to have saved the life of John Smith, one of the founders of Jamestown. She was later kidnapped by the English, converted to Christianity and married the colonist John Rolfe. She came to England in 1617 where she was presented at the court of James I. She is buried at Gravesend, Kent. Artist: Hole. MPG 284

US–Canadian border

Boundary mound built by a detachment of the Royal Engineers, c. 1885. Mounds like this marked the border along the 49th Parallel in the notorious 'badlands' area around the Red River in North Dakota. FO 302/30 (32)

The United States

Declaration of Independence, 1776. Drafted by Thomas Jefferson and others, the declaration was approved by Congress on 4 July and printed that very night by John Dunlop of Philadelphia. One of only twenty-one copies known to have survived, this was enclosed in a letter sent to the Admiralty. ADM 1/487

The Empire

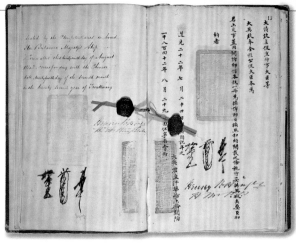

AT ITS HEIGHT Britain's empire covered more than a quarter of the world's land surface – 'the Empire upon which the sun never set'. The public records chronicle its development, how it was administered and its ultimate dissolution, and are a rich source of information for scholars from all over the world: Britain's imperial and international trading interests also involved her in the affairs of innumerable countries beyond her borders.

Hong Kong
Nanking treaty, 1842. Under the terms of the treaty, which ended the three-year Opium War, China gave rights to British traders in five ports and ceded Hong Kong island to Britain.
FO 93/23/1B

BUY EMPIRE GOODS FROM HOME AND OVERSEAS

The Empire
'Highways of Empire', Empire Marketing Board, 1927. After World War I the British empire was at its height. The poster shows its major trade routes.
Artist: MacDonald Gill.
CO 956/537 (2)

Gibraltar
Poster, Empire Marketing Board, 1928. A Royal Navy warship and the Rock of Gibraltar were two powerful symbols of empire. The poster is from the series 'The Empire's Highway to India'. Artist: Charles Pears.
CO 956/688

Sierra Leone
Map of the fortifications on George Island, 1749. British traders were active along the coast of Sierra Leone from the start of the 18th century, and the country was a British colony from 1808 to 1961.
CO 700 Sierra Leone 1B

Colonial allies
'Our Allies the Colonies', 1939–45. Forty-nine British colonies are listed on either side of the central figure. The dissolution of the empire started soon after 1945 as countries gained their independence and joined the British Commonwealth.
INF 13/213 (31)

South Africa
Mrs Waller of Durban, Natal, and her rickshaw driver, 1903. Natal was at that time a separate colony and had been given internal self-government in 1893; it became a founding province of the Union of South Africa in 1910.
Photographer: William Thomas.
COPY 1/464

Work and Play

INNUMERABLE EVERYDAY CONCERNS and pleasures are illuminated by material in the public records. The state began to regulate the working conditions of men and women employed by private companies in the nineteenth century. Leisure activities could become a useful source of 'voluntary' tax revenue – lotteries are an example, both now and 300 years ago.

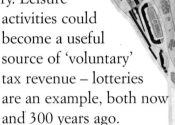

Festival of Britain
Festival gardens poster, 1951. A celebration of the country's achievements, the Festival of Britain was held on the South Bank of the Thames to mark the centenary of the Great Exhibition of 1851, and symbolized British optimism after the hardships of World War II. The festival gardens, facing the river in Battersea Park, were designed by two artists, John Piper and Osbert Lancaster.
WORK 25/223

Cotton industry
Cotton mill workers, 1905. Frank Clarke, who photographed these girls in Manchester, was a supporter of the suffragette movement.
COPY 1/492

Lotteries
Private lottery tickets, 18th century (left). England's first state lottery was established as early as 1567 and draws were held regularly between 1694 and 1768. The late-18th century wooden balls (right) were also probably used in a private lottery.
IR 55/30;
IR 55/28

Regent's Park

John Nash's plan for Regent's Park, 1828. A royal hunting ground until the Parliamentary victory in the Civil War, the park reverted to the Crown in 1811. Nash designed it as a private pleasure ground for the Prince Regent, but it was opened to the public in 1838. MPE 912

Coal miners

Miners at work, Snowdown Colliery, Kent, 1950s. Increasingly strong government regulation of private industry culminated in the nationalization of key industries, such as coal mining in 1947. COAL 80/914

COLOMBO, CEYLON

Dock workers

'Our Trade with the East', Empire Marketing Board poster, 1928. Trade within the empire provided work for dockers in Ceylon (now Sri Lanka) as well as their counterparts in Britain.
Artist: Kenneth D Shoesmith. CO 956/13

Football

Players and directors of the Woolwich Arsenal football team, 1894–5. The club started as the works team of the munitions factory at Woolwich and was the first southern one to gain entry to the Football League. Photographer: Thomas Symmons. COPY 1/419

PRO Publications
Public Record Office
Ruskin Avenue
Kew, Surrey, TW9 4DU

http://www.pro.gov.uk/

© Crown copyright 1998

ISBN 1 873162 71 5

Designed by Roger Hammond

Images available from the PRO
Image Library

A catalogue card for this book is
available from the British Library.

CREDITS

FRONT COVER
The Public Record
Office, Kew. © Hugh
Alexander 1998

Charles II, c.1665.
Illumination of the Stuart
monarch from a plea
roll. KB 27/1837

'Back Them Up!' World
War II Ministry of
Information poster
showing a British cruiser
ramming an Italian
submarine in the
Mediterranean.
Artist: Marc Stone.
INF 13/123/24

Elevation of clock dial
from maps and plans
of the Houses of
Parliament, 19th
century. WORK 29/3284

Churchill, Roosevelt and
Stalin at the Yalta
conference, February
1945. INF 14/447

Illuminated manuscript
(background). Page
from 15th-century Book
of Statutes, Edward III –
Henry VI. E 164/10

BACK COVER
Address presented to
Queen Victoria on the
occasion of her
Diamond Jubilee in

1897 by the Royal
Institute of Painters in
Water Colours. PP 1/303

Perspective view of the
picture gallery at
Buckingham Palace,
from maps and plans of
the royal palaces,
1914. WORK 34/1403

'Bravo Mate, Keep It
Up!' World War II
Ministry of Information
poster. INF 13/213 (43)

Edward II's gift of the
earldom of Cornwall to
Peter Gaveston,
6 August 1307
(background). E 41/460

TITLE PAGE
Domesday Book,
1086. E 31/2

Empire Marketing
Board poster, 1928.
CO 956/13

ABOVE
Charter of Henry II,
c. 1155–60.
E 42/527